# Women's Work

## in pictures

Pictures
to share

for Annie and May, and others like them,
who never had much of a choice.

## Pictures to share

First published in 2006 by
Pictures to Share Community Interest Company,
a UK based social enterprise that publishes
illustrated books for older people.

www.picturestoshare.co.uk

**ISBN 10** 0-9553940-2-3
**ISBN 13** 978-0-9553940-2-7

**Front Cover:** Woman painting her nails 1940's.
Photographic Advertising Ltd Archive/Nat. Museum of Photography,
Film and TV/Science & Society Picture Library
**Endpapers:** Elizabethan Bouquet by Anna Scott from A-Z of Stumpwork.
Country Bumkin Publications, Australia www.countrybumkin.com.au
**Title page:** Detail from Lady in Grey, 1859 by Daniel Macnee (1806-82)
National Gallery of Scotland, Edinburgh/The Bridgeman Art Library
**Back cover:** Detail from The Farm Maid 1887 by Alfred Roll.
Detail from Nun mending shoes by Chris Ware.
Detail from A Laundry Maid Ironing by Henry Robert Morland.

# Women's Work

## in pictures

Edited by Helen J Bate

I've got the children to tend
The clothes to mend
The floor to mop
The food to shop
Then the chicken to fry
The baby to dry
I got company to feed
The garden to weed
I've got shirts to press.
The tots to dress...

Quotation from 'A Woman's Work' taken from 'And Still I Rise'
by Maya Angelou © Maya Angelou/Little, Brown Book Group, London.
Painting: Details from The Ball of Wool by Dorothea Sharp
(1874-1955) Private Collection/ © John Davies Fine Paintings/
The Bridgeman Art Library

# The view of history

that we get through the kitchen window is a more gentle view, not of war and politics, but of family and community and sharing.

Quotation: Julia McWilliams Child (1912-2004)
In Memory and Imagination BPS TV 15th Aug 1993
Main photograph: Katie Davis and her sister-in-law Mrs Burns
working on their milkround in Glebe Street, Chiswick
by Reg Speller. Hulton Archive/Getty Images
Small photograph: Boy at window Lambert/Archive Photos/Getty images

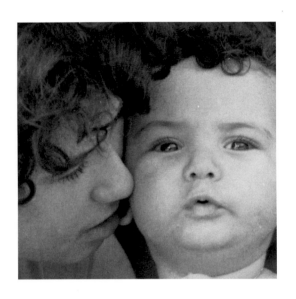

# There is nothing

## as strong as tenderness

Quotation: Saint Francis de Sales,
French saint & bishop of Geneva (1567-1622)
Photographs: Mother Washing Baby © Sefton Samuels FRPS

# It makes the mind very free

when we give up wishing
and only think of bearing
what is laid upon us, and doing
what is given us to do.

Quotation from 'The Mill on the Floss' bk 5 Ch 1, 1860
by George Eliot (Mary Ann Evans) (1819-80)
Painting: A Laundry Maid Ironing by Henry Robert Morland (1716-97)
Lady Lever Art Gallery, National Museums Liverpool

# Amy Johnson

became the first woman to fly solo from England to Australia in 1930, winning £10,000 from the Daily Mail newspaper.

Her plane was a De Havilland Gipsy Moth aircraft nicknamed 'Jason'.

Amy joined the Air Transport Auxiliary as a pilot in World War 2 and died when her plane was lost over the Thames estuary.

Yours very sincerely

# How different,

how very different,
from the home life of
our own dear Queen!

Quotation: Overheard from a member of the audience when
Sarah Bernhardt appeared in the role of Cleopatra in 1892
Photograph: Nun mending shoes by Chris Ware.
Hulton Archive/Getty Images.

# When I talk with other men

I always think of you -
Your words are keener
than their words,
And they are gentler, too.

When I look at other men,
I wish your face were there,
With its gray eyes and dark skin
And tossed black hair.

When I think of other men,
Dreaming alone by day,
The thought of you like a strong wind
Blows the dreams away.

Quotation: 'Other Men' by Sara Teasdale (1884-1933)
Drawing: Seated dancer by Henri de Toulouse-Lautrec (1864-1901)
Pastel on paper. The Bridgemen Art Library/Getty Images
Small photograph: College student by Yellow Dog Productions.
Riser/Getty Images

# Any intelligent woman

who reads the marriage contract
and then goes into it,
deserves all the consequences.

Quotation from My Life by Isadora Duncan (1878-1927)
Painting: Detail from Wedding Morning by J H F Bacon (1865/8-1914)
Lady Lever Art Gallery, National Museums Liverpool

# Mary Holmes receives a peck on the nose

from a jackdaw at the Formakin Animal Training School in Oxfordshire, where she trained animals for show-business appearances.

Photograph by Chris Ware. Hulton Archive/Getty Images

During the 2nd World War
the Silver Cross pram factory
was used to produce aircraft
parts for the war effort.

After the war, the experience
gained was applied to production
methods, and the traditional
plywood pram construction
was replaced with aluminium.

Painting: Detail from Sewing in the Sun 1913
by Brake Baldwin (1885-1915).
The Bridgeman Art Library/Getty Images
Small picture: Spitfire aircraft in flight by Michael Dunning.
Photographer's Choice/Getty Images

# If women are expected to do the same work as men,

we must teach them
the same things.

Quotation: Plato. Greek author & philosopher (427 BC - 347 BC)
Main photograph: Female carpenter by Barbara Peacock/Getty Images
Small photograph by Thurston Hopkins/Hulton Archive/Getty Images

# I saw my grandad late last evening

On a hillside scything hay
Wiped his brow
and gazed about him
Gathering in the day.

Heard screams and laughter
from the orchard
Saw a boy and girl at play
Watched them turn
their heads towards me
Gathering in the day.

And my mother at a window
On some long-forgotten May
Lifts her eyes and smiles upon us
Gathering in the day.

Quotation from 'Gathering in the Days' by Gareth Owen (1936 - )
Copyright © Gareth Owen 1995.
Reproduced by permission of the author c/o Rogers, Coleridge
and White Ltd., 20 Powis Mews, London W I I  I JN.
Painting: The Farm Maid 1887 by Alfred Roll (1846-1919)
Musee d'Orsay, Paris, France/Bridgeman Art Library/Getty Images

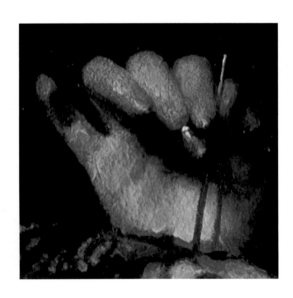

No fine work
can be done
without
**concentration**

# And for tired eyes
every light is too bright,

# and for tired lips
every breath too heavy,

# and for tired ears
every word too much.

Quotation: Georg Büchner (1813-1837) Trans. by Gerhard P. Knapp
Main Photograph: Mother holding infant in bed by George Marks.
Hulton Archive/Getty Images
Small photograph: Comet Kohoutek against the stars.
Evening Standard/Hulton Archive/Getty Images

**Pictures to share**

**Acknowledgements**
Our thanks to the many contributors who have allowed their
text or imagery to be used for a reduced or no fee.
Thanks also to all those who assisted in the development of this
book by helping with or taking part in trials; especially Sally Reid,
Occupational Therapist, of Prospect House Nursing Home,
Malpas, and John Thompson, Activities Co-ordinator
at Crawfords Walk Nursing Home, Chester.

All effort has been made to contact copyright holders.
If you own the copyright for work that is represented, but have
not been contacted, please get in touch via our website.

**Thanks to our sponsors**
The UnLtd Millennium Awards Scheme
The LankellyChase Foundation
The Rayne Foundation
The Cheshire Partnership
Cheshire and Warrington Social Enterprise Partnership

Some quotations have been provided by
'Chambers Dictionary of Quotations',
Chambers Harrap Publishers Ltd, 2005

**Published by**
Pictures to Share Community Interest Company.
Peckforton, Cheshire
**www.picturestoshare.co.uk**

Printed in England by
Burlington Press, 1 Station Road, Foxton CB22 6SA

| 1 | 2 | 3 | 4 | 5 | 6 | 7 | 8 | 9 | 10 |
|---|---|---|---|---|---|---|---|---|---|
| 11 | 12 | 13 | 14 | 15 | 16 | 17 | 18 | 19 | 20 |
| 21 | 22 | 23 | 24 | 25 | 26 | 27 | 28 | 29 | 30 |
| 31 | 32 | 33 | 34 | 35 | 36 | 37 | 38 | 39 | 40 |
| 41 | 42 | 43 | 44 | 45 | 46 | 47 | 48 | 49 | 50 |
| 51 | 52 | 53 | 54 | 55 | 56 | 57 | 58 | 59 | 60 |
| 61 | 62 | 63 | 64 | 65 | 66 | 67 | 68 | 69 | 70 |
| 71 | 72 | 73 | 74 | 75 | 76 | 77 | 78 | 79 | 80 |
| 81 | 82 | 83 | 84 | 85 | 86 | 87 | 88 | 89 | 90 |
| 91 | 92 | 93 | 94 | 95 | 96 | 97 | 98 | 99 | 100 |
| 101 | 102 | 103 | 104 | 105 | 106 | 107 | 108 | 109 | 110 |
| 111 | 112 | 113 | 114 | 115 | 116 | 117 | 118 | 119 | 120 |
| 121 | 122 | 123 | 124 | 125 | 126 | 127 | 128 | 129 | 130 |
| 131 | 132 | 133 | 134 | 135 | 136 | 137 | 138 | 139 | 140 |
| 141 | 142 | 143 | 144 | 145 | 146 | 147 | 148 | 149 | 150 |
| 151 | 152 | 153 | 154 | 155 | 156 | 157 | 158 | 159 | 160 |
| 161 | 162 | 163 | 164 | 165 | 166 | 167 | 168 | 169 | 170 |
| 171 | 172 | 173 | 174 | 175 | 176 | 177 | 178 | 179 | 180 |
| 181 | 182 | 183 | 184 | 185 | 186 | 187 | 188 | 189 | 190 |
| 191 | 192 | 193 | 194 | 195 | 196 | 197 | 198 | 199 | 200 |
| 201 | 202 | 203 | 204 | 205 | 206 | 207 | 208 | 209 | 210 |
| 211 | 212 | 213 | 214 | 215 | 216 | 217 | 218 | 219 | 220 |
| 221 | 222 | 223 | 224 | 225 | 226 | 227 | 228 | 229 | 230 |
| 231 | 232 | 233 | 234 | 235 | 236 | 237 | 238 | 239 | 240 |
| 241 | 242 | 243 | 244 | 245 | 246 | 247 | 248 | 249 | 250 |
| 251 | 252 | 253 | 254 | 255 | 256 | 257 | 258 | 259 | 260 |
| 261 | 262 | 263 | 264 | 265 | 266 | 267 | 268 | 269 | 270 |
| 271 | 272 | 273 | 274 | 275 | 276 | 277 | 278 | 279 | 280 |
| 281 | 282 | 283 | 284 | 285 | 286 | 287 | 288 | 289 | 290 |
| 291 | 292 | 293 | 294 | 295 | 296 | 297 | 298 | 299 | 300 |
| 301 | 302 | 303 | 304 | 305 | 306 | 307 | 308 | 309 | 310 |
| 311 | 312 | 313 | 314 | 315 | 316 | 317 | 318 | 319 | 320 |
| 321 | 322 | 323 | 324 | 325 | 326 | 327 | 328 | 329 | 330 |
| 331 | 332 | 333 | 334 | 335 | 336 | 337 | 338 | 339 | 340 |
| 341 | 342 | 343 | 344 | 345 | 346 | 347 | 348 | 349 | 350 |
| 351 | 352 | 353 | 354 | 355 | 356 | 357 | 358 | 359 | 360 |
| 361 | 362 | 363 | 364 | 365 | 366 | 367 | 368 | 369 | 370 |
| 371 | 372 | 373 | 374 | 375 | 376 | 377 | 378 | 379 | 380 |
| 381 | 382 | 383 | 384 | 385 | 386 | 387 | 388 | 389 | 390 |
| 391 | 392 | 393 | 394 | 395 | 396 | 397 | 398 | 399 | 400 |